Empath

Understanding The Journey of A Highly Sensitive Mindful Soul Filled To The Brim With Empathy

Chloe B. Johnson

The information contained in this book is not intended to replace any treatment. It is still best to seek professional help. This book is only a supplement. The information contained in this book is accurate. It is a product of extensive research. This book was written to the best of the author's knowledge. But, the author should not be held liable for omissions and errors. The photos in this book are taken from stock photo websites.

Upon reading this book, you agree to hold the author harmless against and from any costs or damages that can result from the application of the information provided by this book. This disclaimer applies to any direct or indirect injury or damages caused by the use of the information in this book, whether it's a tort, negligence, contract, or any other cause of legal action.

You agree to accept all the risks of applying the information contained in this book. If needed, consult a doctor to ensure that you're healthy and capable enough to apply and use the strategies presented in this book.

Dedication

This book is dedicated to all the Highly sensitive people I have met through my journeys and with whom I have crossed paths.

What's Next

You will enjoy reading this book, and I am confident that you will find it speaks deep into your soul. You can find more information on my books and myself personally. Go to https://jestmy.com/r/chloebooks

Free Gift

Firstly I want to thank you for making my journey a part of your incredible journey. Studies have shown that most adults find it hard to self improve, but can significantly improve by simply making use of a journal to track and support their progress. So I have decided to offer you a FREE print at home wellness journal. This journal contains 8 different methods to assist you in superior wellness. Go download your free gift now.

https://jestmy.com/r/chloegift

Support Groups

Studies have shown that parallel to journaling and tracking your progress and feelings, sharing your story, and hearing others tell their story has an incredibly positive impact on people. So I have started a group for like-minded people. If you are looking for a group of incredible people who share your experiences and have similar journeys, and would like to share your story, you must join our group today at: https://jestmy.com/r/chloegroup

Contents

INTRODUCTION

Firstly I want to thank you for buying this book and taking a step in the direction of knowledge. May you prosper in your journeys.

We are all born with a certain degree of empathy. For some people, this quality is extremely intense and difficult to manage, leading them to be labelled "highly sensitive" or "empaths." These individuals are often misdiagnosed with conditions such as anxiety or depression because their emotional sensitivities are so pronounced. However, new research is emerging that suggests highly sensitive empaths can actually thrive in life if they learn how to manage their sensitivities properly.

Highly sensitive people (HSP) are a unique breed. They make up only around 15-20 per cent of the population and are known for their heightened intuition, deep empathizing abilities, and propensity for introspection. This makes them incredibly insightful and caring individuals, but can also lead to a lot of stress and overwhelm.

Highly sensitive people have a unique gift: the ability to deeply empathize. This can be a great boon in both personal relationships and work relationships, but it can also feel draining. Take time to reflect on the things that bring you the most energy, and focus on those things! For example, if you love being with animals but are drained by time spent with noisy crowds, do what you can to spend more time around animals. You'll find your energy levels much higher when you do.

Often highly sensitive people get overwhelmed because they forget about themselves—so remember: self-care is important for everyone, especially HSPs! Learn ways to check in with yourself and focus on your needs, then put them into action. This might mean taking a few minutes in the morning to journal before work or taking an hour at night to read a book you love every day. Or maybe it means spending 20 minutes meditating every morning before you start your day. Whatever works for you, make sure you're doing it daily. It will make a world of difference!

The empath differs from a normal person in that they have a stronger ability to read and understand the emotions of others. This can lead them to feel overwhelmed by their own feelings and those around them. An empath may also experience extreme physical symptoms when stressed out or upset.

Some people believe they are empaths because they can easily pick up on the moods of others. Others think they are empaths because of their intense reactions to certain situations. Some even say they are empaths because their intuition tells them what others are feeling.

CAN HIGHLY SENSITIVE EMPATHS THRIVE IN LIFE

If you're a highly sensitive person, chances are you feel things deeply. While this can be wonderful in many ways, it can also mean you need more time and space to process your emotions. By giving yourself permission to explore your emotions and thoughts, you'll be able to better manage them and not let them overwhelm you.

Are you highly sensitive? Most people are, but they don't know it. You might be a highly sensitive empath if you:

-often feel others' emotions
-have been called "too emotional" by those close to you
-have trouble with sensory overload (bright light, loud sounds, strong smells)
-feel "too much" at times when experiencing nature or art.

Highly sensitive people represent a large portion of the population. They are empathic, creative and passionate. There is no right or wrong way to be.

Human beings are all different, and we're all wired in different ways. Some of us are more emotionally sensitive than others, and the more emotionally sensitive we are, the more likely it is that we're born with a trait known as high sensitivity.

What does it mean to be a highly sensitive person? Are there any benefits of being highly sensitive or are people who have this trait cursed?

Empathy is a powerful tool in marketing and sales. There are two types of empathy: cognitive empathy and emotional empathy. The first type is the understanding of someone's mindset and how they think. The second type is the understanding of someone's feelings or emotions about the situation.

Cognitive empathy is important for salespeople to understand because it helps you to understand what your customers want. You can then provide them with that product or service. Emotional empathy is important because it helps you to understand why someone wants something, so you can give them what they need.

Empathy is the glue that binds a group of people together. Empathy can be translated as "feeling into", it is your ability to feel or relate to other people's feelings.

Empathy is a mental concept that has a direct impact on your physical and mental health and well-being. If you are an empath, you need to know how you are able to take on other people's feelings and emotions without them affecting you negatively. For example, as an empath, you may be able to feel what your boss feels when he is angry with you at.

Being an empath has its upsides and downsides. Being able to sense other people's feelings and energy can be a great asset, but being overstimulated by other people's emotions can be overwhelming. This is especially true for highly sensitive empaths.

Highly sensitive empaths have the ability to read people and situations at a deeper level, and they are highly intuitive. They are also creative, empathetic, thoughtful, loyal and generous. But being an empath comes with challenges too. Highly sensitive empaths can be extremely sensitive to other people's emotions and energy. They can feel everything from the pain of others to their own self-doubt.

That said, there are ways HSPs can thrive in life. Here are some examples:

Avoid big crowds:

Since HSPs tend to feel overwhelmed by loud noises, bright lights, and deep stimulation, it's best to avoid being in a large crowd where they may feel overstimulated.

Take time to go within:

HSPs are naturally introspective people; it's just part of who they are. Since they tend to go within more than most people, they need ample time to do so each day. This could be as simple as taking 20 minutes to sit in silence or walking through nature with no distractions.

Use a journal:

Some HSPs struggle with being able to put their thoughts into words that others can understand. A journal is a great tool for these individuals because it gives them a safe space to write out their thoughts without worrying about how   they   will   affect   others

Highly Sensitive Empaths Can Thrive In Life

For a highly sensitive empath, the world can be an overwhelming place. We are bombarded with stimuli from all directions. It is so easy to get lost in your thoughts and feelings when there are so many external factors affecting you.

Understanding That You Are An Empath.
As an empath, you have a deep connection with others and the planet itself. You feel things deeply, sometimes to your own detriment. While this may seem like a burden at times, it also gives you

Learn To Take A Deep Breath.
Sometimes, you simply need to step back and take a deep breath

Understand That You Can't Fix Other People's Problems.
As an empath, it is very easy for you to try and fix other people's problems easy being an empath—it takes strength. You can't fix other people's problems, but you can be there for them and help them find their own solutions.

Understand That You Are Not Responsible For Other People's Feelings.
Being an empath will always be a part of you, but you can learn how to manage these strong feelings

Understand That You Are Not Responsible For Other People's Thoughts.

You are not responsible for other people's thoughts. You can't read minds, and you can't control what other people think. You can only control your own. Many beautiful and kind empaths feel a strong need to fix other people's problems.

Understand That You Are Not Responsible For Other People's Actions.

You can't fix other people. They have to want to change themselves.

You are not responsible for other people's actions.

You can't control what other people do.

You can only control your own.

You are not responsible for other people's actions.

You can't control what other people do.

You can only control your own.

"I'm not responsible for other people's actions. I can only control my own."

Don't Seek Revenge.

Revenge is a negative emotion that hurts you more than it hurts the person you're seeking revenge on. You'll

Understand That You Are Not Responsible For Other People's Actions.

You can't control what other people do. You can only control your own.

Don't Give Up.

If you fail, get back up and try again. It's okay to fail as long as you learn from your mistakes and keep trying.

Don't Let Fear Stop You From Trying New Things.

Fear is a normal part of life, but it shouldn't stop you from trying new things.

Don't Worry About What Other People Think Of You.

The only opinion that matters is your own.

Don't Give Up On Your Dreams.

You may have to take a few steps back before you can move forward, but it's worth it in the end.

Don't Worry About What People Think Of You.

You never know what they're going through.

Don't Give Up On Love.

It's worth the wait and the risk.

Don't Be Afraid To Ask For Help.

Everyone needs a little help sometimes.

Understanding Empaths and Empathy

Empath-Related Problems and How to Overcome Them.

Even though empaths may have an easier time connecting with others and building relationships, some challenges come along with being highly empathic. Let's discuss some of the many empath-related aspects and how to deal with them:

Empaths feel everything!

Empaths tend to be very sensitive to the feelings of others. They can feel the emotions of those around them like physical energy that radiates off of every person they meet. If empaths are in a room full of people who are arguing and having a bad day, they will feel very uncomfortable until the situation is resolved.

Empaths can feel drained by others.

Empaths are highly sensitive to the energy of others, which means they can easily become overwhelmed by the emotions of those around them. This is especially true when empaths are around people who are having a bad day or going through a difficult time. Empaths can feel the negative energy and emotions of others, which makes them feel drained and tired.

Empaths often have to be alone to recharge.

Empaths are highly sensitive people who need a lot of alone time to stay balanced and centred. This is because empaths have a tendency to absorb the energy of others, which can make them feel overwhelmed and exhausted. Empaths need to be alone in order to restore their energy and balance.

Empaths are highly intuitive people who have a strong connection with the spiritual realm.

Empaths are often considered psychic or intuitive because they have a strong connection with the spiritual realm. They are highly sensitive to the energy of others and can often feel when someone is not being truthful or sincere. Empaths also have an innate ability to predict future events, which makes them very good at their jobs.

Empaths are extremely sensitive to the energy of others and their surroundings.

Empaths have a very strong sense of intuition, which is why they can often sense when someone is not being truthful or sincere. They are also highly sensitive to the energy of others and their surroundings, which is why they often feel overwhelmed in large crowds or around people who are not very positive.

Empaths can easily pick up on other people's emotions.

Empaths have the ability to tune into other people's emotions, which is why they often feel overwhelmed in large crowds or around people who are not very positive. This also makes it very easy for empaths to tell when someone is not being truthful or sincere.

Empaths are highly sensitive to the energy of others and their surroundings.

Empaths have a very strong sense of intuition, which is why they can often sense when someone is not being truthful or sincere. They are also very aware of their surroundings and the energy that is being emitted from everything around them.

Empaths feel things more deeply than others do.
Empaths have a tendency to feel emotions on a much deeper level than others. They are also more in touch with their own emotions and the emotions of others.

Empaths often feel like they don't fit in with everyone else.
They feel different and weird, and they often don't understand why.

Empaths are more sensitive to pain than others are.
They feel pain in their own body, and they also feel the pain of others.

Empaths are often more creative than others.
They have a deep connection to the spiritual world, and they often feel like they are part of it.

Empaths have a very deep connection to the spiritual world.
They feel that they are part of it, and they often feel like they are connected to a higher power.

Empaths are often very spiritual people.
They have a deep connection to the spiritual world, and they often feel like they are part of it.

Empaths are often more creative than others.
They have a deep connection to the spiritual world, and they often feel like

they are part of it.

Empaths have a deep connection to animals and plants.

They often feel what the animals and plants are feeling, and they are deeply connected to them.

Empaths are highly intuitive.

They can sense what is going on around them, and they know what others are feeling without being told.

Empaths are deeply compassionate.

They feel the pain of others, and they want to help them feel better.

Empaths have a strong sense of justice.

They believe in fairness, and they will fight for what is right.

Empaths are highly creative.

They uniquely see the world, and they are able to express themselves in a special way.

Empaths are natural healers.

They want to help people feel better, and they have the skills to do it.

Empaths are natural listeners.

They have a gift for listening to people, and they often know exactly what to say to help them feel better.

Empaths are very giving.

They have a hard time saying no, and they want to help others as much as possible.

Empaths feel things deeply.

They often take on the emotions of others. They feel things very deeply, and it is difficult for them to ignore their feelings.

Empaths are not good at lying.

They cannot lie without feeling guilty, and they often tell the truth even when it would be better to lie.

Empaths are good listeners.

They make great friends and partners. They are able to listen to the needs of others, and they do not judge. They are good at helping others feel better about themselves.

Empaths have a hard time being around negative people.

They are very sensitive to negativity, and they cannot tolerate it for very long.

Empaths are good at giving advice.

They do not like to receive it. They do not like being told what to do, and they hate being controlled.

Empaths are always ready to help others.

They often forget to take care of themselves.

Empaths are always in a hurry.

They hate being late for an appointment. They want everything to be on time, and they want to be on time themselves.

Empaths are very independent.

They do not like to depend on other people for anything. They want to make their own decisions, and they want to do everything on their own.

Empaths are very intuitive.

They can sense other people's emotions and feelings. They know when someone is not being honest with them, and they know when someone is telling a lie.

Empaths are very good listeners.

They always try to understand other people's points of view. They do not like to argue with other people, and they do not like to judge other people.

Empaths are very creative.

They have a vivid imagination. They can easily get inspired by things around them, and they can easily come up with new ideas.

Empaths are very good at giving advice.

They usually have a lot of wisdom to share with other people. They know how to listen to other people, and they know how to give them advice in a way that is easy for them to understand.

Empaths are very good at making decisions.

They are usually very decisive. They don't need a lot of time to think about what they want to do, and they don't have a hard time making decisions.

Empaths are very good at seeing the big picture.

They usually have a good sense of what is going on in the world around them. They know how to look at things from different perspectives, and they know

how to take into account all of the factors that are involved in a situation.

Empaths have a very good sense of humour.

They usually know how to make other people laugh. They can be very witty and sarcastic, and they usually have a lot of funny stories to tell.

Empaths are always in tune with the cycles of nature.

They can easily tell you what season it is, just by looking at the trees and the flowers.

Empaths are great listeners.

Empaths are great listeners, and they usually have a lot of patience when it comes to listening to other people's problems.

Empaths are great at giving advice.

Empaths are great at giving advice, especially when it comes to relationships and emotions.

Empaths love animals.

Empaths love animals, and they will do anything to protect them.

Empaths are very creative.

Empaths are very creative, especially when it comes to writing or art.

Empaths are excellent listeners.

Empaths are excellent listeners, and they will always lend an ear to anyone who needs it.

Empaths have a great sense of humour.

Empaths have a great sense of humor, and they will always make you laugh.

Empaths are very passionate people.
Empaths are very passionate people, and they have a hard time controlling their emotions.

Empaths are great at solving other people's problems.
Empaths are great at solving other people's problems, and they will always help you find a solution to your problems.

Empaths are highly intuitive.
Empaths are highly intuitive, and they will always know when something is wrong with you.

Empaths are extremely sensitive to energy.
Empaths are extremely sensitive to energy, and they will always know if someone is lying or not.

Empaths are always the peacemakers.
Empaths are always the peacemakers, and they will never start a fight with anyone.

Empaths are highly perceptive of other peoples feelings.
Empaths are highly perceptive of other people's feelings, and they will always know if someone is upset or not.

Empaths are extremely intuitive.
Empaths are extremely intuitive, and they will always know if someone is being dishonest or not.

Empaths are highly sensitive to the energy of other people.

Empaths are highly sensitive to the energy of other people, and they will always know if someone is in a bad mood or not.

Empaths are highly perceptive of other people's emotions.

Empaths are highly perceptive of other people's emotions, and they will always know if someone is feeling positive or negative emotions.

Empaths are very intuitive of other people's thoughts.

Empaths are very intuitive of other people's thoughts, and they will always know if someone is thinking positive or negative thoughts about them.

Empaths are highly intuitive of other people's intentions.

Empaths are highly intuitive of other people's intentions, and they will always know if someone is thinking positive or negative thoughts about them.

Empaths can be in a room with people they don't know and still sense their emotions.

Empaths can be in a room with people they don't know and still sense their emotions.

Empaths will feel drained after being around certain people.

Empaths will feel drained after being around certain people, and they may even get physically ill.

Empaths can be overwhelmed by large crowds of people.

Empaths can be overwhelmed in large crowds of people.

Empaths can pick up on people's subtle body language.

Empaths can pick up on people's subtle body language, and they are usually very good at reading people.

Empaths are usually very good listeners.

Empaths are usually very good listeners, and they make great friends.

Empaths are highly intuitive.

Empaths are highly intuitive, and they can sense things that others cannot.

Empaths are natural healers.

Empaths are natural healers, and they can often sense the emotions of others.

Empaths are creative and artistic.

Empaths are creative and artistic, and they are usually very good at writing.

Empaths are sensitive to loud noises.

Empaths are sensitive to loud noises, and they cannot tolerate a lot of chaos in their lives.

Empaths are very giving.

Empaths are very giving, and they will often give more than they can afford to give.

Empaths have a lot of love to give.

Empaths have a lot of love to give, and they will often give their love freely without any expectations.

Empaths are very protective of their loved ones.

Empaths are very protective of their loved ones, and they will do whatever it takes to keep them safe.

Empaths are extremely loyal.

Empaths are extremely loyal, and they will remain loyal even when it seems like there is no hope.

Empaths are great listeners.

Empaths are great listeners, and they will listen to you when no one else will.

Empaths are very intuitive.

Empaths are very intuitive, and they will often know what you are thinking without you saying a word.

Empaths are highly creative.

Empaths are highly creative, and they will often come up with unique solutions to problems that others would never think of.

Empaths have a deep connection with animals.

Empaths have a deep connection with animals, and they will often be able to communicate with them on a level that others cannot.

Empaths are natural healers.

Empaths are natural healers and they will often be able to heal others with their hands.

Empaths are good listeners.

Empaths are good listeners, and they will often be able to give you the advice that you need to hear.

Empaths are very spiritual people.

Empaths are very spiritual people, and they will often have a deep connection with the universe.

Empaths are highly intuitive.

Empaths are highly intuitive, and they will often be able to sense things that others cannot.

Empaths are always very calm.

Empaths are always very calm, and they will often be able to remain completely calm.

Understanding And Embracing Your Gift As An Empath

We are all here with a purpose, and as an empath, your purpose is to feel.

You are so much more than just another person walking through the world, trying to make it through the day. You are an empath, and you have been given a gift by the universe to help others heal in ways that most humans can't.

As an empath, you feel everything at a deeper level than those around you. You may have even tried to hide your feelings from others because you've felt that they were too intense for others to handle. But your feelings aren't wrong; in fact, they're what allows you to help others find peace within themselves when things feel overwhelming for them.

Your sensitivity is not a burden—it's a gift. It's what allows you to hold space for others in ways that most people can't. You may feel like you're carrying the weight of the world on your shoulders, but please know that those who come to you for comfort and healing do so because of your gift—not despite it.

To truly embrace your gift as an empath, we recommend practising mindfulness every day in order to stay centred and grounded while still being able to help those around you find their way back. Yoga is an excellent way to achieve mindfulness.

The empath's journey is not always an easy one. Your gift of understanding and feeling other people's emotions and physical sensations can mean that the world often feels overwhelming. It can mean that you are sensitive and empathic to a fault—that you take on too much responsibility for other people's feelings. And it can mean that you are constantly being misperceived as someone who is just a little bit "off" or "weird."

In today's world, we are constantly bombarded by information. The average adult sees up to 3,000 advertisements per day. In the US alone, there are about 200 million registered cars constantly on the move and contributing to traffic congestion. We are overstimulated, and often feel weighed down by our emotions and overwhelmed by our senses.

As an empath or an emotionally sensitive person, this can be especially taxing. You're not just absorbing your own emotions—you're picking up on others' moods as well. But don't let this upset you! Empaths have a special skill that is incredibly magical: they can hear what people say without having to hear it spoken. This is a gift that should be embraced in order to tune into your natural superpower.

This superpower is the ability to hear messages from the universe (or "the other side") through inner voices, sounds, words and music that come spontaneously and seemingly out of nowhere. It's a form of psychic hearing that allows you to receive messages outside of your own sensory experience. Have you ever had a hunch that something was going to happen before it occurred, and then later found out you were right?

SHIELDING YOURSELF AS AN EMPATH

Here are 5 tips for shielding yourself as an empath.

Create a boundary around yourself.

One of the best ways to shield yourself from outside stimuli is to create a boundary around yourself. This means that you should create a physical or emotional barrier between yourself and the rest of the world.

You can do this by closing your eyes, turning away from people, or putting up a mental shield around yourself. The key is to find what works best for you and to use it whenever you need it.

Take some time for YOURSELF.

Whenever you start feeling overwhelmed by everything happening around you, take some time for yourself. This could mean taking a walk outdoors, reading a book, or taking a relaxing bath.

The important thing is to find an activity that allows you to tune out the world and focus on YOU. This will help you to recharge and restore your energy.

Connect with nature.

Another great way to shield yourself as an empath is to connect with nature. This could mean spending time outside in the garden, going for a walk in the park, or simply sitting outside and enjoying the fresh air.

Nature has a way of cleansing and restoring us, so make sure to take advantage of it whenever you can!

Meditate regularly.

If you want a more permanent solution for shielding yourself as an empath, consider meditating regularly. This will help you to create a stronger boundary between yourself and the rest of the world.

Plus, meditation is a great way to calm the mind and restore balance within yourself. So if you're feeling overwhelmed, consider giving it a try!

Seek professional help if needed.

If you find that you are struggling to cope with being an empath, it may be a good idea to seek professional help. A therapist can provide you with support and guidance as you learn to cope with your gifts.

Meditation for a Highly Sensitive Empaths

Highly sensitive empaths can often experience difficulty dealing with the strong emotions of others. It is important to understand how meditation can help you gain control over your feelings and cope better with the overwhelming emotions of others.

Meditation is a common practice for people who have a high level of emotional sensitivity. It helps them to regulate their emotions, cope with the constant onslaught of emotions from other people, and to analyze their own emotions.

The ability to feel others' emotions is called clairsentience, which means 'clear feeling.' Clairsentience is a term that refers to being able to sense or feel the energies or vibrations of other beings around you.

Clairsentience is an ability that many highly sensitive empaths possess in varying degrees, but not all highly sensitive empaths have the ability to feel others' emotions in this way.

The Empath or Highly Sensitive Person (HSP) is a trait that describes the way some people experience the world. It's estimated that about 15-20% of people are HSPs, and although it affects men and women equally, it tends to be more widely understood in women.

What does this have to do with meditation? For those of us who are HSPs, meditation can be a particularly powerful tool for maintaining mental health. By tuning into our bodies' sensations, we can learn to relax on command, which means we're less likely to experience anxiety and other stress-related symptoms. Meditation can also teach us how to navigate our overwhelming emotions without allowing them to take over our lives.

Meditation has been shown to help with self-regulation, stress management, and resilience in the face of trauma—all issues that are intimately connected to the HSE experience. We're not here to tell you that meditation can solve all your problems (because you already know that wouldn't work!), but we do believe that it offers a powerful set of tools that can help you lead a more balanced life with less pain and suffering.

The practise of meditation can be very beneficial for Highly Sensitive Empaths. It is a way to reset your brain and tune out external stimuli, which are often overwhelming for Highly Sensitive Empaths.

Meditation allows you to disconnect from the outside world and feel more completely connected to yourself. In today's busy society, it's easy for Highly Sensitive Empaths (HSEs) to get swept up in the go-go-go mentality and lose touch with their feelings, which are often heightened by a sensitivity to the emotions of others.

When you're feeling anxious or sad, it's important to distance yourself from your emotions and observe them (as if you were just an observer), rather than letting your emotions take over you. When you're feeling overwhelmed by your senses, meditation gives you a way to detach from them and focus on something else instead.

To begin meditating, find a quiet place free from distractions where you can focus solely on your breathing. Feel free to sit or lie down, whichever is more comfortable for you. Begin taking deep breaths, inhaling through your nose and exhaling through your mouth. On each inhale, imagine that you are bringing in all of the positive energy in the world—all of the love and support that exists around you—and on each exhale, imagine that you are releasing all of your stress, anxiety, and negative energy.

Try to keep this cycle going for at least ten minutes—if it helps, set an alarm for yourself so that you don't have to worry about time passing.

Many of the attributes that make someone a Highly Sensitive Empath also make it harder for them to meditate; super-sensitivity can lead to a hyper-awareness of sounds, fidgeting, and other external stimuli. This can make it easy to get distracted and lose focus.

First, it is important to understand that everyone has different ways of approaching meditation. What works for one person will not necessarily work for another, so don't try to force yourself into any particular mould or style. If you have tried meditation before and found it difficult, this doesn't mean you're doing it wrong—it just means that what you were doing didn't work for your unique brain.

So how do you find a style that works for you? First, think about what kind of distractions bother you the most. Is it noise? Movement? Do people walking through the room throw off your rhythm?

Once you've identified what's causing your distractions, think about how these things can be managed in a way that works for your lifestyle and schedule. For example: If noise is your biggest distraction, can you set aside time in the evening when you can be alone and everything is quiet.

When you're feeling anxious or sad, it's important to distance yourself from your emotions and observe them (as if you were just an observer), rather than letting your emotions take over you. When you're feeling overwhelmed by your senses, meditation gives you a way to detach from them and focus on something   else   instead.

A Way To Cultivate Being An Empath

Empathy is a way of being that allows us to understand what others are feeling. It's not just about understanding someone else's emotions but rather feeling them yourself. When we empathize with someone, we can feel their pain, joy, fear, anger, sadness and love. We can even feel other people's thoughts and intentions. This ability to feel what others are feeling is known as empathic intuition.

To get started on being an empath, you're going to need to gather a few essential oils. These essential oils will help you to connect with your emotions and the emotions of others. You'll also need a small potted plant that you can keep on your desk, or somewhere in your home. This plant will represent your emotional state. When it is wilted, your emotional state is at its lowest. When the plant is flourishing and healthy, you are able to be more empathetic and receptive to outside forces. It's important that your plant not be symbolic of any particular person in your life

There are multiple types of plants that work well for this exercise; you should choose one that is easy to care for and requires minimal maintenance. You'll want to pick a plant that doesn't require much sunlight or water, so as not to overwhelm yourself with constant care-taking responsibilities. Choose a plant that will thrive even if you don't give it much attention – because you won't always have time or energy for it. Let your new plant be a symbol of the emotional energy you can expand when needed, but also of how little emotional energy sometimes needs to be expended in order for the job to get done. The less complicated the plant is, the better; choose something like succulents or cacti if you're worried about forgetting about its needs too often.

Start with a small plant that is easy to care for. Each day, care for your plant by watering it and making sure it has enough sunlight. Because you are an empath, this will likely feel like a chore sometimes. You may feel obligated to tend to the needs of the plant because otherwise, it will die. Over time, you may begin to feel resentful of your plant.

But in order to keep this exercise going, you must continue caring for your plant no matter how much you feel you don't want to care for it anymore. You must continue caring for your plant even if you don't think it deserves your attention anymore, or if you feel like there is no point in doing so because the whole thing was a dumb idea anyway. Someday, when you have successfully completed this exercise (i.e., kept the plant alive for at least three months), you can permit yourself to stop caring for your plant. But until then, know that your job is not only to keep yourself happy and healthy – but also this very specific type of plant that only exists on this planet and nowhere else in the universe.

The role of an empath is to help others feel better about themselves, their lives, and the world around them. An empath can do this by listening to people's problems and helping them find solutions to those problems. They are able to connect with people emotionally and mentally, allowing them to understand what they are feeling and thinking. This allows the empath to help people become aware of how they are affecting other people and themselves.

An empath has a natural ability to read the emotions and feelings that others have. They can pick up on these emotions and feelings without being told directly. They are able to sense what someone else is feeling, even if they don't know exactly what it is. They may not always know what to say or do, but they can usually tell if something is wrong or right.

Empaths are often misunderstood. People think that they are weak or crazy. But the truth is that empaths are just different from everyone else. They are sensitive to the needs of others and want to make sure that everyone feels good. They care deeply about other people's well-being and happiness.

An empath is someone highly sensitive to the energy around them. They are very perceptive and intuitive. They have a keen sense of what other people think or feel. This makes them good at reading people, which can be useful in many situations. Empaths also tend to be very compassionate and caring people. Some empaths are able to use their abilities to heal others, while others use their abilities for their own benefit.

Empaths are often misunderstood. People think that they are weak or crazy. But the truth is that empaths are just different from everyone else. They have a natural ability to read the emotions and feelings that others have. They can pick up on these emotions and feelings without being told directly. They are able to sense what someone else is feeling, even if they don't know exactly what it is. This allows them to help people become aware of how they are affecting other people and themselves. By listening to people's problems and helping them find solutions, empaths can help others feel better about themselves, their lives, and the world around them.

Yet, the empath has a unique gift: They can help others understand their own emotions and feelings so they may better figure out what to do. This ability to understand people's emotions, feelings and intentions are what makes them special.

The empath is able to offer compassion and empathy for those around them. They want to be there for others and can often times relate very well with people. The empath wants to help others feel better about themselves, their lives and the world around them.

An empath has a natural ability to read the emotions and feelings that others have. They can pick up on these emotions and feelings without being told directly. They are able to sense what someone else is feeling, even if they don't know exactly what it is. They may not always know what to say or do, but they can usually tell if something is wrong or right.

Empaths do not have to be weak or crazy. They can be strong and confident. They can be loving and caring. They can be successful in whatever they choose to do. They just need to find their own way.

However, it's important for an empath to know that they don't have all the answers. They can't solve every problem or make every decision on their own. It takes a lot of listening, patience and understanding to figure out what is best for them and the people around them. Sometimes, you just need someone else's perspective to help you see what's really going on in your life.

The most important thing for an empath is to learn how to use their empathy in a positive way. If you're constantly worrying about how others feel about you or trying too hard to please everyone, then you're not really being an empath at all! You need balance and moderation in order to be successful as an empath (and person). Being an empath doesn't mean being perfect all the time, either; it means finding your own path while still respecting others and their feelings along the way!

You might be an empath if you've ever felt drained after spending time with someone who has been angry or sad. Or maybe you've felt upset when a friend is crying because it seems so real to you. You could even be an empath if you're constantly trying to put others' feelings before your own in order to help them feel better about themselves.

When an empath is around someone who is upset, it can affect them as well. The empath may feel the same way that the other person does, even if they don't know why this is happening! This is because an empath has a strong sense of empathy, which means that they have an intense awareness of what other people are feeling and thinking about at all times (even when those people aren't aware themselves!).

Practicing Mindfulness as an Empath

Mindful awareness involves being aware of what we think, feel, do and experience while accepting whatever arises moment to moment. In addition to being present, mindful attention includes having interest, compassion, curiosity, appreciation and acceptance. It is through mindfulness meditation that one becomes more compassionate towards oneself and others.

Mindfulness is the practice of being present in the moment. It is the awareness that allows you to notice what is happening right now. Mindfulness is a way of being that is cultivated over time. You can cultivate mindfulness in a number of ways, but the most effective way is through mindfulness meditation. Mindfulness meditation is a form of meditation that emphasizes observing your thoughts, feelings, and sensations without judgment. It is a way of being that helps you to develop self-awareness and compassion for yourself and others. It helps you to be more present, which helps you to become a more effective person.

Mindfulness is the practice of being in the moment. Mindfulness means to be fully present, to live in the moment. Mindfulness is about paying attention to the present moment in a nonjudgmental way. It is about being present with what is, and noticing things as they are. It is about being aware of our thoughts, feelings, and bodily sensations. It is about observing our thoughts and feelings without getting caught up in them. It is about noticing our breath, our body, and our environment. Mindfulness means to be fully present, to live in the moment. Mindfulness is about paying attention to the present moment in a nonjudgmental way. It is about being present with what is, and noticing things as they are. It is about observing our thoughts, feelings, and bodily sensations. It is about observing our thoughts and feelings without getting caught up in them.

Mindfulness is a practice that is becoming increasingly popular in the Western world. This guide will help you understand mindfulness in a practical and spiritual sense. It is written from an empathic perspective, which means it will help you to develop your empathic abilities. This guide will help you to develop your empathic abilities and will give you an understanding of mindfulness in a spiritual sense. It will help you to develop your empathic abilities and will give you an understanding of mindfulness in a spiritual sense.

Mindfulness is a practice that can be done anytime, anywhere, and with any-thing. It is a way to be more aware of the present moment. Mindfulness is an attitude of acceptance, non-judgment, and a willingness to see things as they are. The word "mindfulness" is derived from the Pali word, sati, which means "to remember." The essence of mindfulness is to be aware of the present moment, without judgement, without wishing or hoping for something else, and without clinging to the past or dreading the future. Mindfulness is a practice that cultivates the ability to be fully present and to be fully aware of what is happening in the present moment.

Mindfulness is a skill that can be cultivated and developed through practice. Mindfulness is the practice of paying attention to your experience in the present moment in a non-judgmental way. It is a way of seeing the world and yourself in a different way. It is a way of being in the world. Mindfulness is a practice of developing the ability to focus on the present moment, without judgment. It is a way of learning to be with and accept your feelings, thoughts, and perceptions. Mindfulness is the practice of being with your feelings, thoughts, and perceptions, without judgment. It is a way of seeing the world and yourself in a different way. It is a way of being in the world. Mindfulness is a practice of developing the ability to focus on the present moment, without judgment.

The most important thing that mindfulness does for you is it allows you to become more aware of the present moment. When you are aware of the present moment, you are more likely to live in the moment and not let your mind run off into the future or the past. It is important to practice mindfulness because it helps you be in the present and not let the present slip away. You can use mindfulness to help you become more aware of your life and your relationships with others.

Mindfulness is a way of living that is gentle and compassionate to yourself and the world around you. It is a way of being that is free from judgment, free from preconceptions, and free from bias. It is a way of being that is self-reflective and self-aware. It is a way of being that is non-judgmental and non-attached. Mindfulness is a way of being that is free from the ego, free from the ego's need to control and manipulate. Mindfulness is a way of being that is free from the ego's need to possess and own. It is a way of being that is free from the ego's need to be right and to be powerful.

Mindfulness is a practice that can be used to cultivate a sense of presence and awareness, reduce stress, and develop qualities of the mind such as attention, kindness, compassion, and equanimity. It is a practice that can be done anywhere and can be practised in any setting. Mindfulness is the intentional and non-judgmental observation of one's thoughts and feelings in the present moment. Mindfulness can be practised in a formal setting or everyday life. It can be practiced in formal settings such as meditation or in informal settings such as walking, eating, or working. In this guide, I will be discussing the practice of mindfulness in a spiritual context.

As a spiritual practice, mindfulness is a way of being in the present moment. It is about noticing what is happening, with the awareness that this is the only moment that exists. It is about being fully present in the moment, not just in the body, but in the mind and emotions. Mindfulness helps us to be more aware of the moment and to live more fully in the present.

Mindful awareness. Mindful awareness is a state of mind that allows us to be aware and aware of our surroundings. We are aware that we are in a world that is very different from our own. We must be aware of this difference. We need to be mindful awareness to be able to cope with it.

TYPES OF EMPATHS

There are two types of empaths: emotional (intuitive) and sensory (intellectual).

Emotional empaths are often called intuitive empaths. Emotional empaths tend to show up in the world as gentle, kind, and sensitive. They feel other people's emotions deeply, and they tend to be more easily affected by the moods of others. These empaths have a strong sense of intuition. They can arrive at deep realizations without having to go through the process of analyzing them intellectually.

They are the classic "feelers" of the world. They tend to feel the emotions of others very strongly, in both a positive and negative sense. They might even take on these emotions as their own and have trouble distinguishing between their own feelings and those they're absorbing from other people. They tend to be very empathetic and compassionate people, even though they can also be overwhelmed by negative emotions such as anger or sadness.

They are able to sense the emotional landscape of a room by simply being in it. They feel other people's pain in their own bodies. They often experience this information as an overpowering flood of feelings that they must work hard to filter out.

Sensory empaths are often called intellectual empaths or empathic intuitive. Sensory empaths are characterized by their intellectuality and rationality. They are logical thinkers who are able to process information quickly and efficiently. These empaths have a high level of functioning in their five senses—they can notice even the smallest details in their environments with acute precision.

They experience the world through their five senses, but everything is amplified for them. They have an acute sense of sight, hearing, taste, touch, and smell—so much so that they can read subtle signals that most people miss. The world is very loud and bright to sensory empaths, but they are able to filter out what they don't want or need to focus on with great determination and ease.

Unlike emotional empaths, these empaths have a hard time reading people's feelings, but they often have an uncanny ability to know what's going on in someone's mind intellectually.

Because they are so sensitive to intellectual input that they often can't tell the difference between their thoughts and those of other people around them, they tend to be extremely insightful individuals who understand how other people think better than anyone else around them.

People often confuse empaths with narcissists or sociopaths. While this may seem to be the case at first glance, it's important to remember that empaths have good intentions. They want to help others, not harm them. They may also struggle with being unable to separate their feelings from those of other people, which can make them seem unpredictable or unreasonable.

Neuroimaging studies show that the posterior cingulate cortex in empaths is significantly thicker than in non-empaths. The posterior cingulate cortex in empaths also shows heightened responses to emotional stimuli.

Empaths have a strong capacity for repression that allows them to cope with their environment with as little stress as possible. When empaths cannot be alone and escape from the world, they resort to fantasy worlds and daydreaming. Section: The more emotionally attuned during childhood, the more emotionally attuned during adulthood and vice versa.

Family plays a role in determining who is an empath. Empaths can feel how others feel by simply being around them or feeling near them. For example, if an employee or customer is angry or has a bad day, the empath will feel their emotions associated with those negative experiences reverberating through their own bodies and minds.

Empaths feel the same way. For example: a customer will feel anger when someone else says "you're not getting what you deserve"? Similarly, a customer may feel empathy when one disagrees with her work and she finds he's the reason why. An emotional empath may also feel that she's being a jerk and that it is okay for others to hurt her. An empath may also feel empathy when something she does makes her feel uncomfortable. Examples: her boss's employee asked her to get work that day, which is not an empath's job. An empath may feel that she's feeling inferior when asked "why don't you get work that day?"

Empaths work to define a person or thing and do as much as possible. In part that means recognizing which areas of an empath's personality are important and not just ignoring the non-empathic parts.

For example: a person who is "just about to be murdered," the empath who wants to take her own life to take it, will feel pain and pain that is difficult to imagine and so, it is helpful to empathize with her.

Research suggests that empathy can develop because of people's early experiences with emotions within their family upbringing. For example, someone who was neglected during childhood may be more empathetic toward other people because they are able to relate to others' feelings of being unwanted or unloved.

Empathy is a useful trait as it allows us to help others in need without putting ourselves at risk; however, some people have trouble understanding how their own feelings influence their interactions with others. In this book we will explore different kinds of empathy and why it matters

Conclusion

So, how do sensitive empaths thrive in life? One word: empathy. Research has shown that highly sensitive empaths are often very good listeners and caretakers, traits that can put empaths in high demand professionally, personally, and civically. Highly sensitive empaths just need to learn how to manage their extra abilities so that they can live life in balance and be happy.

If you recognize any of these traits in yourself, it is likely that you are a highly sensitive empath. There is nothing inherently wrong with this, but it is difficult to deal with your intense empathy and the emotions of those around you. One way to help cope with these emotions is by educating yourself and learning how to manage your energy levels. It will take a great deal of time and effort, but you do have the ability to lead a successful life as a highly sensitive empath if you find the proper coping mechanisms for yourself.

HSPs and empaths alike need a strong foundation, both cognitively and emotionally, to combat overwhelming empathy in an unfiltered society constantly bombarding us with other people's strong emotions. So, if you are an HSP or empath, I hope this helps you to understand your sensitivity and that it is not just something that should be feared but is a powerful quality of being truly human.

THE AUTHOR

Chloe is a middle aged local activist who enjoys helping old ladies across the road, fitness and human psychology. She is energetic and giving, but can also be very cowardly and a bit untidy. She has a degree in philosophy, politics and economics. She is allergic to milk(go figure). She grew up in a middle-class neighbourhood. She was raised by her father, her mother having left when she was young. Ever since her early teen years, Chloe has always been fascinated by the psychology of the human mind, and all the journeys it takes people on. Being a non-confronting pacifist wrapped into an empathetic blanket, Chloe has always experienced the power of her mind in the most interesting combinations imaginable.